ONE YEAR

AROUND the WORLD

BY CINDY TRUMBORE

For Douglas, who likes holidays.

Modern Curriculum Press

An Imprint of Pearson Learning
299 Jefferson Road, P.O. Box 480
Parsippany, NJ 07054 - 0480

Internet address:
http://www.pearsonlearning.com

Credits

Illustrations: 20: Yoshiya Saito. 21: Chi Chung.

Photos: Front Cover: Ed Pritchard/Tony Stone Images. 5: David Young-Wolff/Tony Stone Images. 8–9: Thierry Prat/Sygma. 11: Dinodia Picture Agency. 14: M. Otero/AP Wide World. 15: Jodi Cobb/National Geographic Society. 19: Phil Schermeister/National Geographic Society. 22: Shizuo Kambayashi/AP Wide World. 24, 25: Michael Newman/PhotoEdit. 26: Joe Viesti/The Viesti Collection. 27: Richard Vogel/AP Wide World. 28: Kathy Sloane. 32: Jerome R. Black/Oregon Exotics-Subzero to Subtropical Nursery. 35: Sakchai Lalit/AP Wide World. 37: Glen Allison/Tony Stone Images. 38: Sakchai Lalit/AP Wide World. 40–41: David Young-Wolff/PhotoEdit. 42: ©Blair Seitz/Photo Researchers, Inc. 44: Joe Viesti/The Viesti Collection. 45: Suraj N. Sharma/Dinodia Picture Agency. 46: Glen Allison/Tony Stone Images.

Design by Design 5 and Agatha Jaspon

ISBN: 0-7652-0885-7

4 5 6 7 8 9 10 MA 05 04 03 02 01 00

Contents

T 42815

Annie Robbins

Sharon Lalav

Omar Desai

Ali Sina

Lydia Wu

Dang Sook

Han Kim

CHAPTER 1

Happy New Year!

Rose Parade "Falconry" float that won the Judges' Special Award (1995)

"Happy New Year!" What do you think of when you hear those words? Do you think of Times Square, where thousands of people gather to watch the giant ball drop at midnight? What about football games and fancy parades? Those things belong to the American New Year's Day, on January 1.

Maybe the new year reminds you of other things. Eating apples dipped in honey is part of the New Year's celebration for some people in America. Others look forward to a present of money in a red envelope. These New Year's customs were brought to our country from other lands.

People celebrate New Year's with different customs.

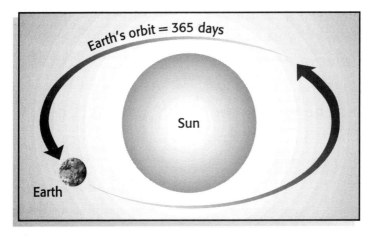

The earth takes one year, or 365 days, to orbit the sun.

New Year's Day is the most widely celebrated holiday in the world. It is also the oldest. People were welcoming the new year 4,000 years ago. Thousands of years ago, people didn't know that the earth travels around the sun. They didn't understand that spring always follows winter. When the cold weather went away and sunny skies came back, they celebrated.

January 1 marks the beginning of a new year called a solar year. *Solar* means "sun." It takes the earth 365 days, or one year, to travel around the sun. The solar new year celebrates the earth completing one orbit, or circle, around the sun.

Different groups of people today welcome the new year in their own special way. They also celebrate at different times of the year. In America, as well as in some other countries around the world, people often have two New Year's. One comes on January 1 and another on their special New Year holiday.

Chinese New Year's celebration

Some people celebrate the new year at the time of the first new moon of winter. We call this holiday the lunar new year. Lunar new year celebrations usually fall in either January or February. Many Asian people, including the Chinese and Vietnamese, celebrate the lunar new year.

For others, the new year comes in the spring. In Iran, the New Year's holiday is called Nowruz (noh ROOZ). That means "new day." It falls on the first days of spring, in March. On this holiday, seeds that have grown into sprouts are a reminder that spring always comes again.

In Thailand, New Year's also comes in the spring, on April 13. It is called Songkran (sahng KRAHN).

On Nowruz, sprouts show that spring is here.

A Diwali lamp

For Jewish people everywhere, the new year comes in the fall. The holiday is called Rosh Hashanah (rahsh hah SHAH nah). It lasts for two days.

In India, New Year's is also celebrated in the fall. The holiday is called Diwali (dih WAH lee). That means "rows of lights." People decorate their houses with tiny lamps at Diwali.

Holidays are a way for people to celebrate things that are important to them. Which New Year's customs belong only to one group? Which customs are shared by everyone? Let's take a look at how children from some different countries celebrate the new year to find out.

New Year's Notes

At New Year's we think about the old year and the new one. January, the first month of our calendar, gets its name from this idea. It is named after Janus, a Roman god with two faces. One face looks backward, the other looks forward.

CHAPTER 2

New Year's in America

Hi! My name is Annie Robbins, and I live in Alabama. On New Year's Eve, I go to First Night with my family. Many communities all over the United States celebrate the new year with a First Night celebration. First Night is a New Year's celebration for the whole family. Different kinds of entertainment like puppet shows, short plays, music, and dances are performed in different places in the center of town.

First we decide what acts we want to see. Then my family walks from place to place to watch the performances. I like the dancing best. My little sister likes the puppet shows, and my parents love all the music.

Some First Night celebrations end with a fireworks display. Sometimes we watch the fireworks. Sometimes we do what many other people do. We go home and watch the big party in Times Square in New York City on television.

New York City must be the noisiest place in America on New Year's Eve!

On New Year's the ball drops in Times Square.

Thousands of people gather in Times Square to watch the "ball lowering." The ball weighs more than 500 pounds and is six feet wide. Its bright lights glitter and shine.

At 11:59 P.M. on New Year's Eve, the ball begins to drop down a tall pole. It reaches the bottom right at 12:00. The people in the crowd count down the seconds and cheer loudly at midnight.

New Year's Eve in Times Square

On New Year's Day, my parents ask me about my New Year's resolutions. A resolution is a plan for making yourself better in the new year. I'm trying to be nicer to my sister. I also want to practice my violin more.

At lunchtime on New Year's Day, we eat a special dish called Hoppin' John. It is said to have begun with African slaves on southern plantations. People in the South still eat it today.

New Year's resolutions are plans for the new year.

Hoppin' John is made with black-eyed peas and rice. Salt pork and spices help to make it taste good. Eating Hoppin' John on New Year's Day is supposed to bring you good luck all year.

Making noise is part of bringing in the new year.

New Year's Notes

Making noise at midnight on New Year's Eve is a custom all around the world. People sing, blow horns, ring bells, and set off fireworks. The custom began long ago, when it was thought that making noise would drive away evil spirits.

CHAPTER 3

The Chinese New Year

My name is Lydia Wu. My family is Chinese American. We live in Houston, Texas. My great-grandparents came to America from China. We celebrate New Year's twice—once on January 1 and again at the Chinese New Year.

We start getting ready for the Chinese New Year holiday about a month before it begins. The first thing is to clean the house from top to bottom. I help with the sweeping. We have to finish our cleaning by the last day of the old year. Nobody wants to sweep on New Year's Day. That would sweep away the good luck that comes in with the new year.

Chinese people have celebrated the new year for thousands of years. Most of our customs come from long ago. Some of the customs are very serious, like the respect we show to people who have died. Others are just plain fun.

One of my favorite customs is the hong bao (hahng bow) packets. These are envelopes with money inside. Parents and relatives give them to children. The envelopes are always red, which is a lucky color. The money is always an even number. Odd numbers are unlucky!

Hong bao packets are fun to get on the Chinese New Year.

恭喜發財

Chinese characters for
Gong hay fat choy

Many Chinese American families have a big reunion dinner on New Year's Eve. Relatives who have not seen each other in a while have a good time sharing a meal together. My big brother even comes home from college to be there.

As guests are greeted, they hear the words *Gong hay fat choy* (gahng hee faht choy). That means "Have a happy and wealthy new year."

The foods that are served at this big feast all have a special meaning. The names for many of the dishes sound the same as Chinese words that mean good luck. We always have fish. The word for fish in Chinese sounds like a Chinese word that means "a lot of plenty."

1995
1983
1996
1984
1994
1982
1997
1985
1993
1981
1998
1986
1992
1980
1999
1987
1991
1979
2000
1988
1990
1978
1989
1977

豬 鼠 牛 虎 兔 龍 蛇 馬 羊 猴 雞 狗

Find the year you were born on this Chinese zodiac.
What animal are you?

Chinese people name each year after an animal. There are only 12 names, so it's easy to remember which is which.

An old Chinese story says that long ago the animals had a great race. The rat finished first, then the ox, then the tiger, and so on through 12 animals. People born in a certain year are supposed to be like that animal. You could be a rat, an ox, a tiger, a hare, a dragon, or a snake. Or you could be a horse, a sheep, a monkey, a rooster, a dog, or a pig.

Chinese dragon

On New Year's Day and the days that follow, there are big parades. Long, long dragons and lions with giant heads walk through the streets. Two people work each lion, while up to 50 people may be inside the dragon costume.

The celebrations last for as long as 15 days in some places. That shows how important this holiday is to Chinese people.

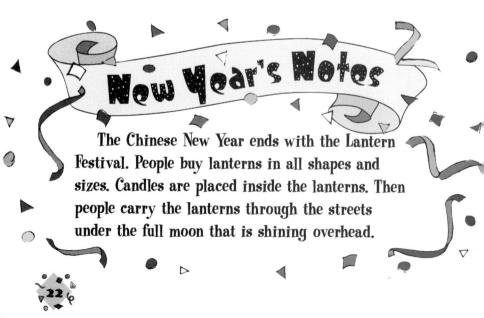

New Year's Notes

The Chinese New Year ends with the Lantern Festival. People buy lanterns in all shapes and sizes. Candles are placed inside the lanterns. Then people carry the lanterns through the streets under the full moon that is shining overhead.

Tet: The Vietnamese New Year

Hi, I'm Han Kim, and I live in California. My parents came to this country from Vietnam before I was born.

The Vietnamese New Year is called Tet and is usually celebrated in February. Since Tet is such a special holiday, people spend a lot of time preparing.

Many people scrub their homes from top to bottom. Then they decorate with plum blossoms. Some people buy new clothes to wear. At Tet, people like to wear red and yellow, the colors of the Vietnamese flag.

Honoring your ancestors is an important custom at Tet. Special tables are set up to remember those who have passed away.

Photographs of relatives are placed on the table along with fruit, flowers, and many different foods. Candles and sweet-smelling incense are on the table, too. The candles are reminders of the sun and the moon. The incense stands for the stars.

Because Tet is the start of a new year, it is a good time to correct mistakes, forgive people, and pay money owed to others. It is also thought to be a good time to get married.

Tet table setting

A family welcomes the honored first visitor during Tet.

People believe that the happiness they feel during Tet will stay with them for the rest of the year and throughout their years together.

Flowers are also important during Tet because it is the beginning of spring. Besides putting flowers inside their homes, some people decorate the outside of their houses, too. They use cherry, plum, peach, and apricot blossoms.

Families get together on New Year's Eve. A big meal is served, with many special foods.

Many people like to eat earth cakes. Earth cakes are rice cakes stuffed with mung beans and pork. It is said that a prince created them once for the people of Vietnam. He used foods that all people could afford to buy.

People also eat dried watermelon seeds that are colored red with food coloring. When you eat them, your lips and fingers turn red. Since red is a lucky color, the belief is that good luck stays with you. People also snack on candied fruit and ginger at Tet.

Tet foods

Planting a kumquat tree

Some families plant kumquat (KUM kwaht) trees during Tet. Every part of the tree has a special meaning for someone in the family. The golden orangelike fruit stands for the family's ancestors. The unripe green fruit is for the grandparents. The fragrant flowers represent the parents. The flower buds are for the children, and the new leaves stand for the grandchildren.

A grandmother gives her grandson a red money envelope during Tet.

Guests are always greeted with the words *Chuc Mung Nam Moi* (chook mung nahm moy). That means, "Happy New Year."

Another custom at Tet that all Vietnamese children love is receiving lucky red envelopes of money. These envelopes are called *li xi* (lee see). They are usually given to the children by grown-up friends and relatives.

Tet lasts for three days. It is especially important for people to be nice to each other during this time. If people frown, they might feel unhappy for the whole year. Everyone spends a lot of time smiling.

Han Kim extends the greeting, "Chuc Mung Nam Moi."

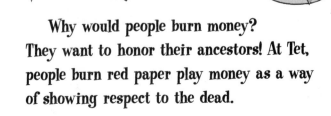

New Year's Notes

Why would people burn money? They want to honor their ancestors! At Tet, people burn red paper play money as a way of showing respect to the dead.

Nowruz:
New Year's in Iran

My name is Ali Sina, and I live in Iran. Our New Year's holiday comes in March. It is called Nowruz.

People start getting ready for Nowruz a few weeks before the holiday begins. Homes are cleaned, people often get new clothes, special foods that can be made ahead of time are prepared, and sprouts begin to grow from seeds that are planted.

On the last Wednesday before the new year, we have a special tradition. We light bonfires in public places. Then people leap over the flames! The fire and light stand for goodness. They light the way to the new year.

There is a special saying for jumping over the fire. People say, "Give me your beautiful red color, and take my pale color away!"

This night is called Fire Wednesday. It is said that you can guess your future on Fire Wednesday. You stand on a street corner and listen to the people walking past. Their words will answer your questions.

On Fire Wednesday children walk through the streets banging on pots and pans with spoons. This is done to scare away bad luck!

Banging pots and pans on Fire Wednesday

Lotus tree fruit

On Nowruz Eve, families gather for a big meal. On the table are seven special dishes. Each one begins with the Arabic letter *S*. One is a sweet pudding made with sprouts. Another is the sweet, dried fruit of the lotus tree. The fruit is supposed to be so good that it helps people to fall in love.

On New Year's Day, children get presents. People say, "May you live a hundred years!" We eat a special meal of rice mixed with herbs and served with fish. It is a fun holiday, and eating lots of cookies makes it even sweeter!

New Year's Notes

A legend from Iran says that the earth shakes at the new year. An egg and a mirror are placed on the table at Nowruz. Families put the egg on the mirror and wait to see it move. Sometimes cannons are shot off to help the egg do its job.

CHAPTER 6

Songkran: New Year's in Thailand

My name is Dang Sook, and I live in Thailand. Songkran is the name of the New Year's festival here. Songkran begins on April 13 and lasts for three days.

The night before the festival begins, Thai families clean their homes. Rubbish and worn-out clothes are thrown away so that they don't bring bad luck in the new year.

In the late morning on Songkran Day, the Bicycle Procession is held. A parade of girls wearing beautiful costumes and holding brightly painted umbrellas ride bicycles through town.

In the afternoon on Songkran Day, statues are driven through town on cars with beautiful decorations. People sprinkle water on the statues for good luck. Boys and girls usually lead the parade. Children dance and play music.

Songkran parade

Water is an important part of the Songkran holiday. People splash water on family and friends to give them good luck. Some people carry buckets of water. Children chase each other with spray bottles or throw buckets of water. Some people throw ice water. The water always feels good because in Thailand, the New Year's festival comes during the hottest part of the year.

Some people play tricks with water at Songkran. They wait at a busy street corner with spray bottles, cups, and buckets. When anyone on a motorcycle comes by—splash! Other people ride in the back of pickup trucks with barrels of water. They dump water on anybody they see. Everyone gets wet at Songkran, but it's all in fun.

Songkran is also a time for showing kindness. As part of the festival, gifts of rice, fruit, and other foods are brought to the monks at the temple. Many people honor the older people in their families. Gifts are given to the older family members, and sweet-smelling water is poured on their hands.

People throw water to celebrate Songkran.

During Songkran, people set birds free.

Everyone is kind to animals on this holiday. People buy birds in the market. During Songkran, they open the birds' cages and set them free. People also carry fish to ponds and streams. The fish, too, are set free.

New Year's Notes

The custom of setting fish free on Songkran started many years ago. After the rainy season, the rainwater dried up. Fish were trapped in pools of water. Farmers saved the fish and let them go on Songkran.

CHAPTER 7

Rosh Hashanah: The Jewish New Year

My name is Sharon Lalav, and I live in New Jersey. My family is Jewish. We celebrate New Year's on January 1, like everybody in America. We also celebrate Rosh Hashanah in the fall. That's the Jewish New Year.

Sometimes my grandparents from Israel come to visit for Rosh Hashanah. In their country, Rosh Hashanah is the only holiday that is kept for two days. That shows how important it is.

Rosh Hashanah means "head of the year." It is a time to think and to plan.

People think about what they have done in the past year. They plan how to make the new year even better.

At Rosh Hashanah, people wish their friends and relatives *L'shanah tovah* (leh shah NAH toh VAH), which means, "May a good year be recorded for you." This comes from a Jewish tradition. It says that at the new year, your future for the coming year is written in the Book of Life.

The foods that are eaten at Rosh Hashanah have a special meaning. People dip apple slices in honey and eat them so that they will have a sweet new year. A round loaf of bread called a *challah* (HAHL ah) is always on the table. Its circular shape shows that the new year always comes around to a new beginning.

Challah, apples, and
honey for Rosh Hashanah

Rabbi J. Wohlberg blows an ancient ram's horn.

On Rosh Hashanah, people usually go to temple. A horn called a *shofar* (SHOH fahr) is always blown at the service. The shofar is one of the oldest of all instruments. It is made from a hollow ram's horn. It tells the people that the new year has begun.

New Year's Notes

Another name for Rosh Hashanah is Day of Blowing the Shofar. This instrument can be made from the horn of a goat or a sheep. Jewish people have been using shofars for over 5,000 years.

CHAPTER 8

Diwali: New Year's in India

Hi! I'm Omar Desai, and I live in India. In India the New Year's celebration is called Diwali. It comes in the fall, just before the new moon.

To get ready for Diwali, people scrub their homes. Many people give the outside of their homes a fresh coat of white paint. Sometimes people decorate the floors and doors of their homes with special designs called *rangoli* (rahn GOH lee). The paint for the rangoli is made from rice flour.

Many people buy bright, colorful new clothes. Old ones are given away.

Diwali is named for the tiny clay lamps that are burned on this holiday. Some people use candles or electric lights.

Another name for Diwali is the Festival of Lights. The lights celebrate stories from the Hindu religion. Light drives away the dark. The bright lights remind people that kindness and wisdom drive away evil.

Many people open their windows at Diwali. Open windows are a sign of welcome to good fortune and wealth.

The Festival of Lights

Diwali lamps

On the first day of Diwali, people wake up very early. They bathe with warm water and oil and then dress in new clothes. Next, they eat a big breakfast, including lots of sweets.

In India, just before dawn during the Diwali celebration, lots of people set off fireworks. The air is filled with booms and bangs. Smoke hangs over the streets as the sun comes up.

At noon, people eat a big festival lunch. Families enjoy the meal together. Then they go out to visit friends and relatives. Gifts and sweets are given and received. At night, the lamps are lit again. They will burn all through the night.

The Diwali celebrations usually last for five days. Each day has its own special customs. Diwali celebrations are slightly different in different parts of India. How Diwali is celebrated depends on where people live. Throughout India, Diwali is a time of great joy.

New Year's Notes

Sweets are everywhere at Diwali. People send boxes of candy and dried fruits to their friends. Favorite candies are made of sugar and coconut. If you get a box of sweets, you send another one back. That keeps the people who sell the special treats busy!

Diwali candy

Happy New Year!

Good luck, good food, good friends, good thoughts, and good fun—these things are a part of everyone's New Year's. However you celebrate the oldest of holidays, it is sure to be one of the most joyful times of your year. So "Gong hay fat choy" … may you live a hundred years … and Happy New Year!

Glossary

ancestor (AN ses tur) a relative who lived a long time ago

celebrate (SEL uh brayt) to take part in special activities that show a day or a time is important

custom (KUS tum) an action that is done now because it was done in the past

decorate (DEK uh rayt) to make something beautiful with bright colors, ribbons, and other trimmings

festival (FES tuh vul) a special party that celebrates an important or happy event

lunar (LOO nur) anything having to do with the moon

procession (proh SEH shun) a group of people moving in an organized way, usually for a ceremony

resolution (rez uh LOO shun) a plan to act in a certain way

respect (rih SPEKT) to show with words or actions that someone is important

tradition (truh DIHSH un) custom or belief that has been handed down from generation to generation